Historical Timeline Figures

The Ultimate Hands-on History Activity for All Ages

By Liberty Wiggers

Published by Little Liberty Publications
Nancy, KY 42544

Acknowledgements

Cover Design:
Michelle E. Wiggers

Editors:
Cindy Wiggers, Maggie Hogan, Michael Kelley, Jane Willis

Hand Drawn Artwork:
Jeanne Wiggers

Tech Support:
Bonnie & Dennis Schwindel, Patty Vanoven

Historical Timeline Figures

The Ultimate Hands-On History Activity for All Ages

First Edition
Copyright © 1999, 2000 Michelle E. Wiggers (Little Liberty Publications)

Published by Little Liberty Publications Nancy, KY 42544
Printed in the United States of America
Library of Congress Catalog Card Number: 99-71654
ISBN: 0-9702403-1-7 (previously ISBN 0-9663722-2-0)

To order or distribute this book contact:
Geography Matters, Inc.
P.O. Box 92 • Nancy, KY 42544
(800) 426-4650

Historical Timeline Figures

The Ultimate Hands-on History Activity for All Ages

Table of Contents

TIMELINE INFORMATION.............................. 5

INSTRUCTIONS..................................... 6

    GAME INSTRUCTIONS........................... 8

    SCORE CARD.................................. 9

NOTEBOOK TIMELINE TO REPRODUCE............. 1 0

TIMELINE FIGURES................................ 1 1

    AFRICA...................................... 1 1

    ASIA.. 1 2

    THE AMERICAS.............................. 1 4

    EUROPE..................................... 1 9

    MIDDLE EAST............................... 2 6

    GENERIC FIGURES........................... 2 7

WHO AM I? GAME CARDS........................ 3 2

CHRONOLOGICAL LIST OF DATES................. 5 2

INDEX.. 5 5

ABOUT THE AUTHOR............................ 5 7

ORDERING INFORMATION........................ 5 7

THIS BOOK IS DEDICATED TO MY MOTHER
FOR NEVER LETTING ME QUIT.
THANKS!

Timeline Information

Remarkable Benefits of Timelines

- Terrific fun, as well as educational.
- Increases understanding of history.
- Improves historical perspective like no other teaching tool.
- Increases excitement at seeing a wonderful visual representation of history.
- Helps students see the "big picture" of how one historical event leads to another.
- Improves critical thinking skills by drawing conclusions from connecting chronological events.
- Benefits all learning styles when using timelines with timeline figures.
- Awakens the brain's memory capacity through visual reminders and hands-on action.

Student Generated Timelines

Student-generated (also called "activity") timelines begin essentially blank. Students add information to the timeline as they learn. Topics may include history, science, literature, fine arts and more. As a subject is studied, add new information to the timeline by:
- Writing in words or short phrases.
- Drawing or pasting in pictures.
- Adding ready-made figures such as those included in this book.

The more frequently the timeline is used, the greater the learning value. It's gratifying to see the timeline develop throughout the year(s)!

Using the Timeline

There are at least four types of activity timelines. Each type has its benefits and its limitations. Select and adapt the style(s) that best suit your teaching needs. Regardless of what style you choose, the method of placing information on the timeline is the same. Record information as it is learned and add any other dates of importance as reference points. Check the index for the time period you are studying and cut out the important figures/events for that era. Students then apply these to the timeline as appropriate. Artistic kids may enjoy drawing and designing their own figures.

Four Types of Timelines

Take these ideas and see what works best for your students.

- Record important events on file cards and file them in a file box in chronological order. (There is no need to "save" room for future studies since cards can be placed before or after any card in the box.) Color-code the cards. Although this method is more difficult for younger children or for those who need to "see" the chronology in a linear fashion, it works well for those who like strict organization and have space limitations.

• Another popular style makes use of a timeline in strips that stretch across the room (down the hall, up the stairs....). This is wonderful for those who need to see historical events in a linear fashion and can be a fun classroom or family project. Stretch time-line strips zig-zag down one wall to show the flow of history. If you have limited wall space, this is not the best method for you!

• If "seeing" historic events depicted chronologically is important, but space is at a premium, there's a terrific poster style activity timeline available from Geography Matters, Inc. The figures in this book were designed to fit easily within the spaces of their Mark-It Timeline of History. The laminated version can also be cut into strips and stretched across the wall, if you choose. Write on the laminate with Vis-a-Vis overhead projector pens. Photograph it at the end of your study and then wipe it off to begin again, or leave the labeling on the timeline and add to it each year.

• Another popular style of student-generated timeline is the notebook format. Each page turned is another view into history. This type is easy to use, can be carried anywhere, and provides an opportunity for the student to record events in more detail. It's exciting to see a student drawing conclusions after seeing events depicted on his personal timeline. (See the cover for an example.) Copy the reproducible notebook timeline on page 10, make 30 or more double-sided copies, three hole punch and place in a three-ring binder. Each page can represent 10, 20, 25, 50 years or however many you'd like. Some pages may represent more and some less. It's easy to add pages in between as new information is learned throughout the year(s). The drawback: students can only "see" one section of history at a time.

Using These Fantastic Figures

These detailed figures add great variety to any timeline. Of course, no set of timeline figures includes pictures of EVERY historical event. That would be impossible! Check the alphabetical index or chronological listing to see if the subject you are studying is represented by a figure. If not, allow students the opportunity to create their own figures. They will probably remember the event even better, having designed the figure themselves.

You can leave the timeline figures in the book and cut them out as you use them, but we suggest a bit of preparation to make the daily use of them more spontaneous. Remove each perforated page and cover with contact paper, lamination or clear packing tape (the "poor man's lamination") to add durability. Place pages in a file in page number order along with the index to make finding the figures easier. File "Who Am I?" card sheets and score sheet in a separate file, or leave bound in the book until ready to use. Now, when the opportunity arises to use the figures select the ones that fit your study, cut them out and attach to your timeline.

Attach the figures permanently or temporarily. Our favorite way is to use removable glue sticks. Place the glue on the back of the figure and press the figure onto the map or timeline where needed. This glue allows for moving and removing the figure as needed. (It works like the popular Post-It™ notes.) You can also use a one inch strip of tape rolled sticky side out.

Occasionally, break away from your general timeline and make a detailed timeline to examine events up close. For example, while involved in a study of the Civil War, make a timeline of the individual battles. Then have the student choose a figure or two to represent the Civil War when you go back to the general timeline.

Timeline figures really spice up a map! Stick Caesar Augustus in Rome or add the Magna Carta to England! Or place the figure along the border or in the ocean and attach a string or draw a line from it to the place of importance.

Terrific Features

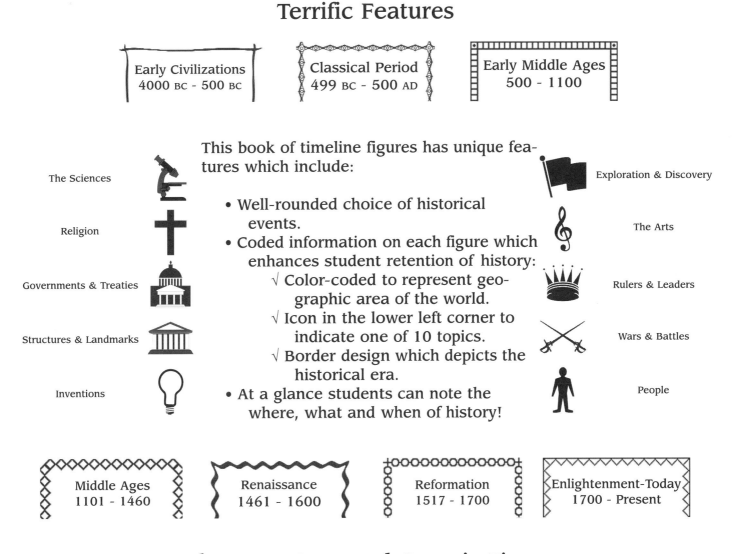

Early Civilizations
4000 BC - 500 BC

Classical Period
499 BC - 500 AD

Early Middle Ages
500 - 1100

The Sciences

Religion

Governments & Treaties

Structures & Landmarks

Inventions

This book of timeline figures has unique features which include:

- Well-rounded choice of historical events.
- Coded information on each figure which enhances student retention of history:
    √ Color-coded to represent geographic area of the world.
    √ Icon in the lower left corner to indicate one of 10 topics.
    √ Border design which depicts the historical era.
- At a glance students can note the where, what and when of history!

Exploration & Discovery

The Arts

Rulers & Leaders

Wars & Battles

People

Middle Ages
1101 - 1460

Renaissance
1461 - 1600

Reformation
1517 - 1700

Enlightenment-Today
1700 - Present

Make-Your-Own and Generic Figures

A great array of generic figures has been included to encourage students to individualize their own unique figures. Kids enjoy making their own. This is done with student-drawn pictures, computer graphics or pictures cut from magazines or copied from books. Color code and duplicate the icons and border designs (or use the blank border figures provided) and voila - customized figures!

Game Instructions
Who Am I?

For two or more players.

To Play:

1. Copy the "Who Am I?" answer sheets and cut them out. Give each player one sheet.

2. Cut out "Who Am I?" cards and shuffle them.

3. Designate one player as questioner. Questioner draws a card from the top of the pile and reads first clue. Players write their answers on the first line. The second clue is given, and players write their second guess on the next line. Continue until all clues are given. If a player is sure of the answer he may use the same answer on the next line.

4 When all clues are given the questioner gives the correct answer. The player to the left of the questioner is the new questioner on the next round and continues to rotate to the left.

To Score:

Score 5 points for answering correctly on the first clue.
4 points for a correct answer on the second clue.
3 points for a correct answer on the third clue.
2 points for a correct answer on the fourth clue.
1 point for a correct answer on the fifth clue.

Note: Not all cards have 5 clues. If a player has answered right more than once for the same card the highest point is scored. He does not receive points for each time he is right.

To Win:

Keep score for each player until one of the players earns 50 points.

Optional Rules:

This game can be played by giving only one player all clues on the card and scoring when he gets the answer correct. A new card is drawn for the next player.

Before or After?

For two players. Use the timeline figures as cards in this game.

To Play:

1. Deal 5 cards to each player. Place the rest of the cards face down as the draw pile. Select a player to go first.

2. The first player selects one card from her hand and says to the other player, "Tell me an event that happened before..." and reads the event, NOT the date, on the chosen card. (She may choose to ask for an event that happened either BEFORE or AFTER the event on her chosen card.)

3. The second player chooses a card from his own hand that names an event that he believes happened before and reads it aloud.

4. If the second player was right he keeps both his card and his opponent's card for scoring later. The first player must take a new card from the draw pile and add it to her hand.

5. If the second player is wrong he must take a card from the draw pile and add it to his hand. The first player keeps both cards for scoring later. Cards kept for scoring are placed aside to count at the end of the game.

6. Now it is the second player's turn to ask his opponent. Play continues as in rules 2-5 until one player is out of cards.

To Win:

Score points by counting cards kept. Each card counts as one point. Each card left in the hand at the end of the game counts as one point against the total score. The player with the most points is the winner.

Optional Rules:

This game can be played with more than 2 players if each person asks the "before" or "after" question to the person to his left. That person becomes the questioner on the next turn.

WHO AM I ?

5 ☐ _____
4 ☐ _____
3 ☐ _____
2 ☐ _____
1 ☐ _____

WHO AM I ?

5 ☐ _____
4 ☐ _____
3 ☐ _____
2 ☐ _____
1 ☐ _____

WHO AM I ?

5 ☐ _____
4 ☐ _____
3 ☐ _____
2 ☐ _____
1 ☐ _____

WHO AM I ?

5 ☐ _____
4 ☐ _____
3 ☐ _____
2 ☐ _____
1 ☐ _____

WHO AM I ?

5 ☐ _____
4 ☐ _____
3 ☐ _____
2 ☐ _____
1 ☐ _____

WHO AM I ?

5 ☐ _____
4 ☐ _____
3 ☐ _____
2 ☐ _____
1 ☐ _____

WHO AM I ?

5 ☐ _____
4 ☐ _____
3 ☐ _____
2 ☐ _____
1 ☐ _____

WHO AM I ?

5 ☐ _____
4 ☐ _____
3 ☐ _____
2 ☐ _____
1 ☐ _____

WHO AM I ?

5 ☐ _____
4 ☐ _____
3 ☐ _____
2 ☐ _____
1 ☐ _____

WHO AM I ?

5 ☐ _____
4 ☐ _____
3 ☐ _____
2 ☐ _____
1 ☐ _____

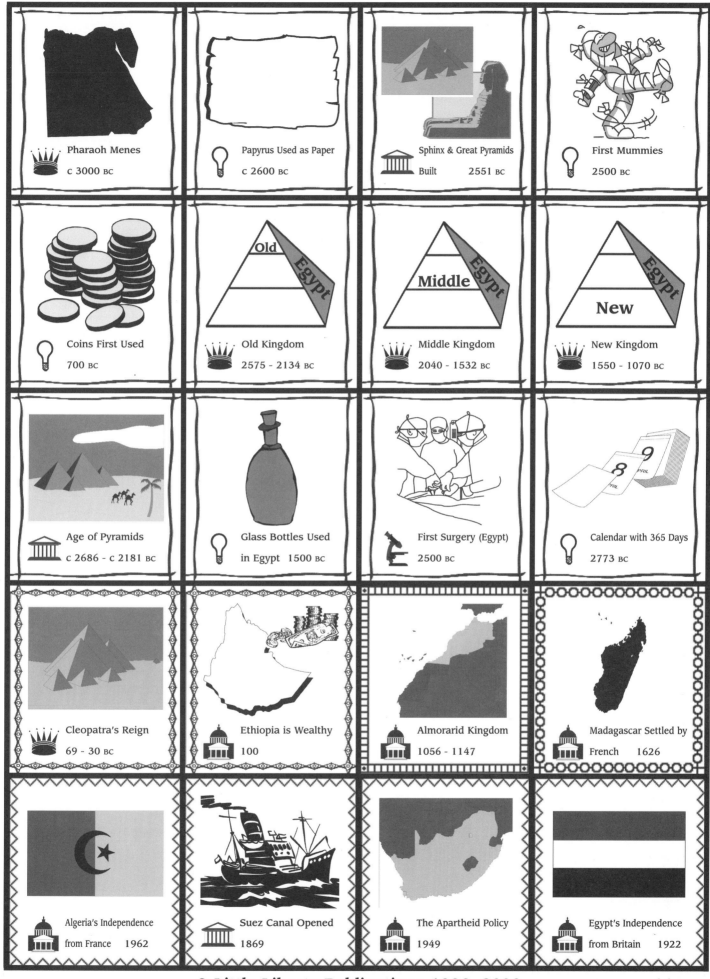

Pharaoh Menes
c 3000 BC

Papyrus Used as Paper
c 2600 BC

Sphinx & Great Pyramids Built
2551 BC

First Mummies
2500 BC

Coins First Used
700 BC

Old Kingdom
2575 - 2134 BC

Middle Kingdom
2040 - 1532 BC

New Kingdom
1550 - 1070 BC

Age of Pyramids
c 2686 - c 2181 BC

Glass Bottles Used in Egypt
1500 BC

First Surgery (Egypt)
2500 BC

Calendar with 365 Days
2773 BC

Cleopatra's Reign
69 - 30 BC

Ethiopia is Wealthy
100

Almorarid Kingdom
1056 - 1147

Madagascar Settled by French
1626

Algeria's Independence from France
1962

Suez Canal Opened
1869

The Apartheid Policy
1949

Egypt's Independence from Britain
1922

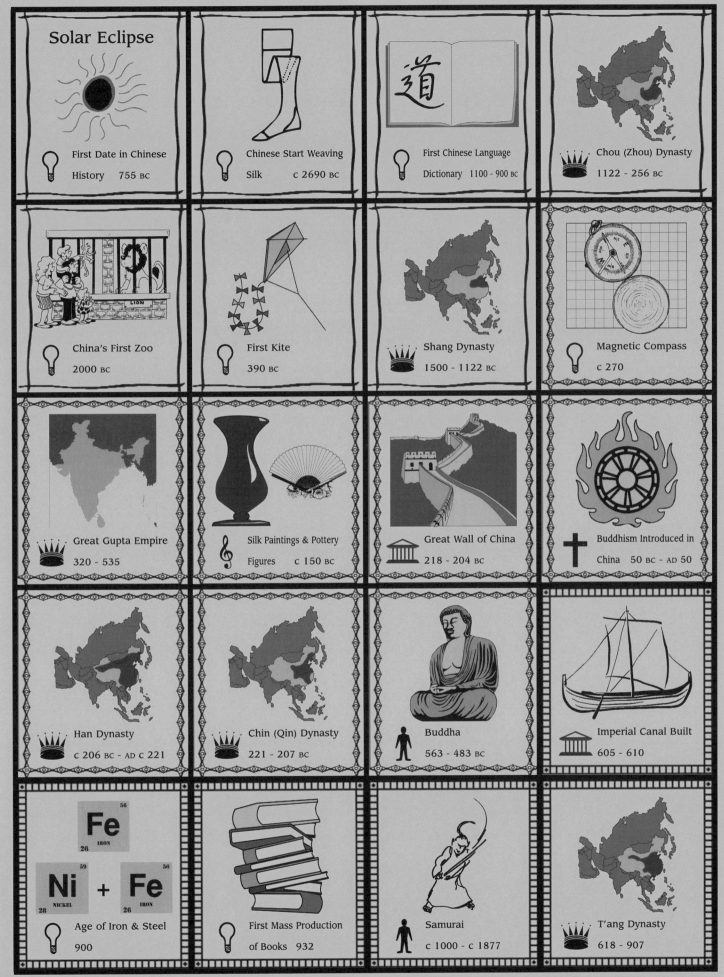

Solar Eclipse

First Date in Chinese History   755 BC

Chinese Start Weaving Silk   c 2690 BC

First Chinese Language Dictionary   1100 - 900 BC

Chou (Zhou) Dynasty   1122 - 256 BC

China's First Zoo   2000 BC

First Kite   390 BC

Shang Dynasty   1500 - 1122 BC

Magnetic Compass   c 270

Great Gupta Empire   320 - 535

Silk Paintings & Pottery Figures   c 150 BC

Great Wall of China   218 - 204 BC

Buddhism Introduced in China   50 BC - AD 50

Han Dynasty   c 206 BC - AD c 221

Chin (Qin) Dynasty   221 - 207 BC

Buddha   563 - 483 BC

Imperial Canal Built   605 - 610

Age of Iron & Steel   900

First Mass Production of Books   932

Samurai   c 1000 - c 1877

T'ang Dynasty   618 - 907

Song Dynasty
960 - 1279

Wooden Blocks for Printing
(China)   593

Genghis Khan
1167 - 1227

Mongol Empire
1279 - 1368

Rockets Used in Battle
1232

Ming Dynasty
1368 - 1644

Peter the Great
1689 - 1725

Mongul Empire
1527 - 1803

Taj Mahal Built
1629 - 1650

JAPAN

Russia

Russo-Japanese War
1904 - 1905

Vladimir Lenin
1870 - 1924

Bolshevik Revolution
1917

People's Republic of
China   1946

Opium War
1839 - 1860

Empress Tzu Hui
1862 - 1908

Mahatma Gandhi
1869 - 1948

Manchu Dynasty
1644 - 1912

BRITAIN, FRANCE,
& TURKEY

Russia

Crimean War
1854 - 1856

Communist
Party

Karl Marx
1818 - 1883

Confucius
551 - 479 BC

First Day in Mayan Calendar 3372 BC

Mayan Golden Age 300 - 600

Tenochtitlan Founded 1325

African Slaves in America 1502

Hernan Cortes 1485 - 1547

Hernando de Soto 1500 - 1542

Virginia Colony Founded 1607

Pilgrims Reach Cape Cod 1620

Salem Witch Trials 1692

Boston Tea Party 1773

Revolutionary War 1776 - 1783

The Declaration of Independence 1776

Treaty of Paris 1783

George Washington 1789 - 1797

California Gold Rush 1849

UNION Confederates Civil War 1861 - 1865

Lewis & Clark Expedition 1804 - 1806

Thomas Edison 1847 - 1931

Airplane Invented 1903

Japanese Attack Pearl Harbor 1941

14

Henry Hudson
? - 1611

Quakers Settle Pennsylvania
1682

First College (Harvard)
Founded   1636

Abortion Legalized
1973

First Space Shuttle
1981

The Telephone
1875

Titanic Sinks
1912

Prohibition
1919

Government Programs
The New Deal
1933 - 1945

Polio Vaccination
1954

Prayer from Schools
1962

Northwest Ordinance
1787

Indians Become American
Citizens   1924

Booker T. Washington
1856 - 1915

U.S. War with Mexico
1846 - 1848

Louisiana Purchase
1803

Transcontinental Railroad
1869

Pony Express
1860 - 1861

Homestead Act
1862

Cotton Gin
1793

Golden Gate Bridge 1937

Statue of Liberty 1886

First Mickey Mouse Cartoon 1928

First Traffic Light 1914

Henry Ford 1863 - 1947

Radio Broadcasting in U.S.A. 1920

Color TV 1950

Clara Barton 1821 - 1912

Man Walks on Moon 1969

Panama Canal Finished 1914

Martin Luther King Jr. 1929 - 1968

The Alamo 1836

U.S. Stock Market Crashes 1929

The Great Depression 1929 - 1932

Atom Bomb First Used 1945

Monroe Doctrine 1823

Salvation Army Founded 1865

Sequoya 1770 - 1843

Simon Bolivar 1783 - 1830

Albert Einstein 1879 - 1955

John Adams
1797 - 1801

Thomas Jefferson
1801 - 1809

James Madison
1809 - 1817

James Monroe
1817 - 1825

John Quincy Adams
1825 - 1829

Andrew Jackson
1829 - 1837

Martin Van Buren
1837 - 1841

William Harrison
1841

John Tyler
1841 - 1845

James Polk
1845 - 1849

Zachary Taylor
1849 -1850

Millard Fillmore
1850 - 1853

Franklin Pierce
1853 - 1857

James Buchanan
1857 - 1861

Abraham Lincoln
1861 - 1865

Andrew Johnson
1865 - 1869

Ulysses Grant
1869 - 1877

Rutherford Hayes
1877 - 1881

James Garfield
1881

Chester Arthur
1881 - 1885

Grover Cleveland
1885 - 1889 & 1893 - 1897

Benjamin Harrison
1889 - 1893

William McKinley
1897 - 1901

Theodore Roosevelt
1901 - 1909

William Taft
1909 - 1913

Woodrow Wilson
1913 - 1921

Warren Harding
1921 - 1923

Calvin Coolidge
1923 - 1929

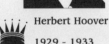
Herbert Hoover
1929 - 1933

Franklin Roosevelt
1933 - 1945

Harry Truman
1945 - 1953

Dwight Eisenhower
1953 - 1961

John Kennedy
1961 - 1963

Lyndon Johnson
1963 - 1969

Richard Nixon
1969 - 1974

Gerald Ford
1974 - 1977

James Carter
1977 - 1981

Ronald Reagan
1981 - 1989

George Bush
1989 - 1993

William Clinton
1993 - ?

Leonardo da Vinci
1452 - 1519

Marco Polo
1254 - 1324

Paper First Made
c 1150

The Inquisition Begins
1233

Canterbury Tales
1388

Movable Type Used
1440

FRANCE
England
Hundred Years' War
1337 - 1453

Brother Sun
Sister Moon
St. Francis of Assisi
1182 - 1226

Bible Now in English
1380

Black Plague
1347 - 1353

Richard the Lion Hearted
1157 - 1199

Popes Dominated by French   1309 - 1377

Magnifying Glass
1266

Byzantine Empire
395 - 1453

Joan of Arc
1412 - 1431

Pablo Picasso
1881 - 1973

King John
Magna Carta Signed
1215

Leaning Tower of Pisa
1174

Sir Walter Raleigh
c 1552 - 1618

Ireland
James Connoly
1870 - 1916

Trojan Wars
c 1250 - 1240 BC

Iliad & Odyssey
c 700 BC

Stonehenge
2700 BC

First Olympic Games
776 BC

Athens 1st Democracy
508 BC

John Calvin
1509 - 1564

Nicolaus Copernicus
1473 - 1543

Mary Queen of Scots
1542 - 1587

Archimedes
c 287 - 212 BC

Constantine
c 280 - 337

Marc Antony
c 83 - 30 BC

Philip II
382 - 336 BC

Ptolemy
90 - 168

First Persecution
54 - 68

Emperor Nero
37 - 68

Hippocrates
c 460 - 377 BC

Legendary King Arthur
c 503

The First Pope
42

Last Roman Emperor
Dethroned 476

The League of Nations
1919

20

Microscope Invented
1590

Spanish Armada Defeated
1588

Johann Sebastian Bach
1685 - 1750

Isaac Newton
1642 - 1727

Pilgrim's Progress
1678

King James Bible
1611

Puritan Revolution (England)
1640

The Reformation Starts
c 1516

First Surgery
1528

Galileo's Telescope
1610

CATHOLICS

Protestants

Thirty Years' War
1618 - 1648

PARLIAMENT

King Charles

English Civil War
1642 - 1648

Louis XIV of France
1638 - 1715

Great Fire of London
1666

William Tyndale
c 1494 - 1536

John Wycliffe
c 1330 - 1384

War of the Roses
1455 - 1485

$a^2 + b^2 = c^2$

Pythagoras
508? - 497 BC

The "Chunnel"
1987

C ommonwealth of

I ndependent

S tates

The CIS (Russia)
1991

Parthenon
477 - 432 BC

SPARTA

Athens

Peloponnesian War
431 - 404 BC

GREEKS

Persians

Persian War
c 490 - 479 BC

ROMANS

Carthage

Punic Wars
264 - 146 BC

Alexander's Empire
Divided   323 - 319 BC

Aristotle
384 - 322 BC

Socrates
469 - 399 BC

Plato
427 - 347 BC

Rome Destroyed by Fire
64

Concrete First Used
in Rome c 200 BC

Julian Calendar
c 45 BC

Alexander the Great
356 - 323 BC

Greek Classical Period
480 BC

Golden Age of Athens
477 - 405 BC

Hannibal
247 - 183 BC

Julius Caesar
100 - 44 BC

ROME

Roman Empire
31 BC - AD 476

ROME

Roman Empire Divided
395

Octavian (Caesar Agustus)
63 BC - AD 14

John Wesley
1703 - 1791

William Shakespeare
1564 - 1616

Ponce de Leon
1460 - 1521

First Watch
1504

Bartholomeu Dias
c 1450 - 1500

Modern Globe
1492

Galileo Galilee
1564 - 1642

Spain Established
1478

Holland's Independence
1587

Christopher Columbus
1451 - 1506

Spanish Inquisition
Starts   1478

Ferdinand & Isabella
1469 - 1516

Henry VIII Separates from
the Church   1529

Michelangelo Buonarroti
1475 - 1564

Henry VII Converts to
Catholicism 1598

Henry VIII
1509 - 1547

Council of Trent
1545

Ferdinand Magellan
1480 - 1521

Martin Luther
1483 - 1546

Scientific Revolution
1543

Queen Elizabeth
1558 - 1603

Vikings Settle Iceland
874

Lief Ericsson Discovers
North America   1003

Pope Nicolas I
858 - 867

Otto I of Germany
936 - 973

The Crusades
1096 - 1204

Charlemagne
771 - 841

Pope Gregory VII Challenges
Henry VI   1077

Treaty of Verdun
843

New Holy Roman Empire
962 - 1806

West   East
Catholic Church Divides
1054

Battle of Hastings
1066

William the Conqueror
1027 - 1087

Florence Nightingale
1820 - 1910

NORTH
ATLANTIC
TREATY
ORGANIZATION
NATO
1949

Francis Ferdinand
? - 1914

Benito Mussolini
1883 - 1945

D - Day
1944

Miracle of Dunkirk
1940

Munich Agreement
1938

YOUNG
MEN'S
CHRISTIAN
ASSOCIATION
YMCA Founded
1844

Eiffel Tower
1889

Balkan Wars
1829 - 1913

Greek Independence
1829

BRITAIN

France

Seven Years' War
1756 - 1763

DANGER POISON GAS

Poison Gas Used in War
1915

Lusitania Sinks
1915

Tanks Used in Battle
1916

Berlin Wall Built
1961

Ludwig Von Beethoven
1770 - 1827

Napoleon Bonaparte
1769 - 1821

Captain James Cook
1728 - 1779

GERMANY

France

Franco - Prussian War
1870 - 1871

ALLIES

Central Powers

World War I
1914 - 1918

Adolf Hitler
1889 - 1945

Spanish Civil War
1936 - 1939

ALLIES

Axis

World War II
1939 - 1945

French Revolution
1789 - 1799

FRANCE   HUNGRY

GERMANY   ITALY

The Triple Alliance
1882 - 1915

FRANCE   RUSSIA

UNTIED KINGDOM

The Triple Entente
1890 - 1915

Treaty of Versailles
1919

Hammurabi's Reign
1792 - 1750 BC

Earliest Known Map
c 3800 BC

Bronze First Used
c 3760 BC

Writing Appears
c 3200 BC

Wheeled Vehicles
c 3000 BC

First Iron Objects Made
c 3000 BC

Basis for Modern
Alphabet c 2000 BC

Windmills Used
600 BC

The Hanging Gardens
580 BC

N. Kingdom of Israel
Destroyed 722 BC

Fall of Babylon
539 BC

Cyrus of Persia
? - 529 BC

Birth of Jesus
c 4

Parchment Replaces Stone
Tablets   460 BC

Jerusalem Falls to Crusaders
1099

Mohammed (Muhammad)
570 - 631

Islam Introduced
622

Ottoman Empire
c 1300 - 1918

Persian Gulf War
1991

Resettlement of Israel
1909

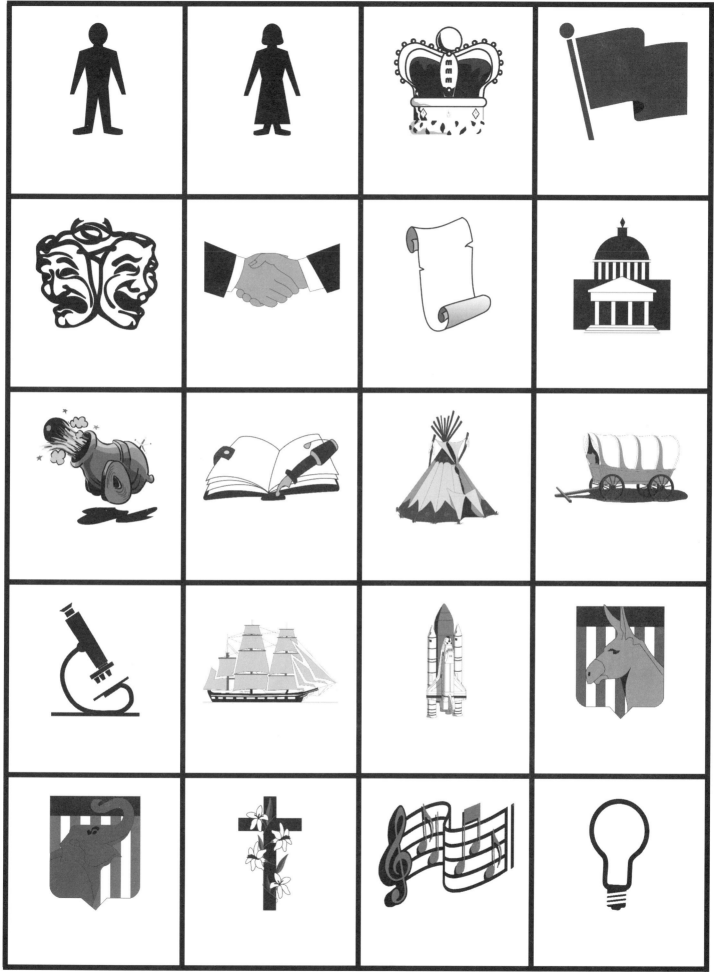

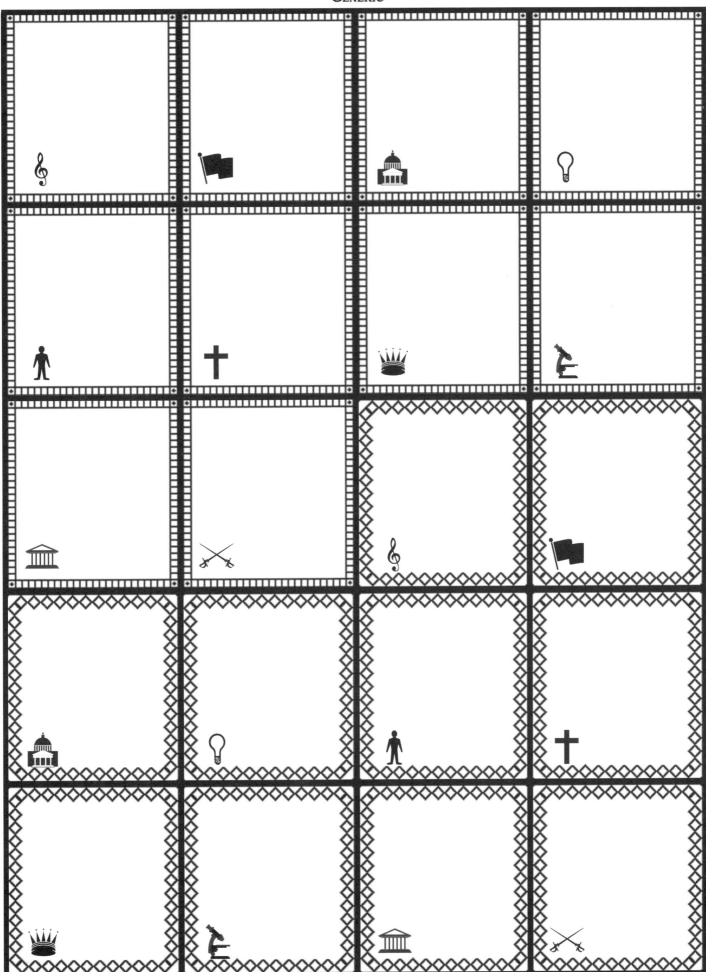

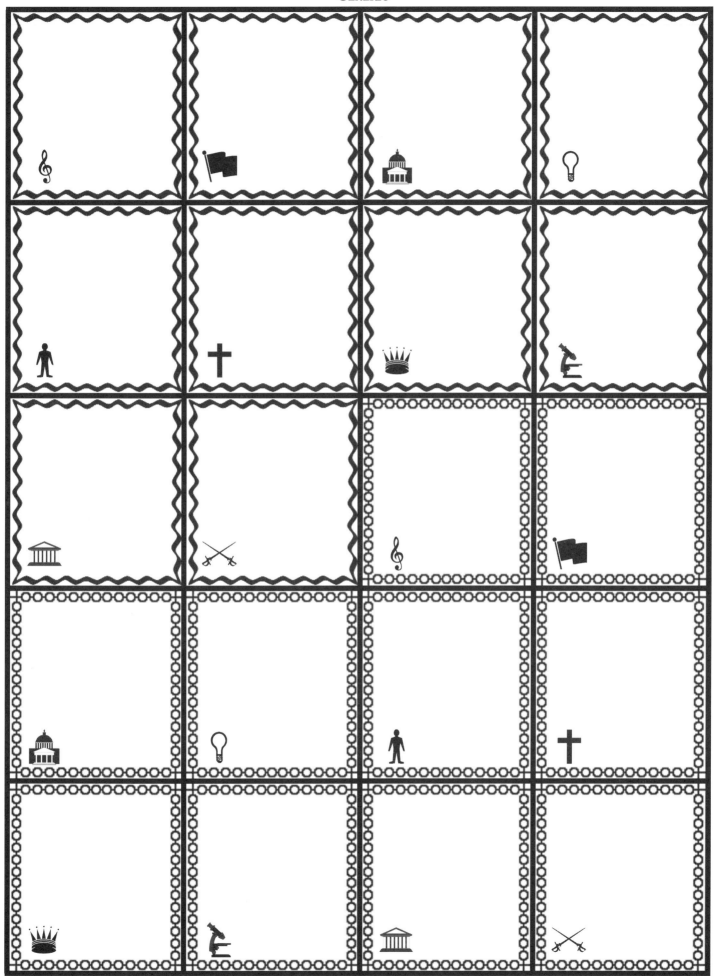

OUR FAMILY HERITAGE

OUR FAMILY HERITAGE

OUR FAMILY HERITAGE

OUR FAMILY HERITAGE

OUR FAMILY HERITAGE

OUR FAMILY HERITAGE

OUR FAMILY HERITAGE

OUR FAMILY HERITAGE

OUR FAMILY HERITAGE

OUR FAMILY HERITAGE

WHO AM I?

- I was a ten year war.
- I was fought between the Mycenaean and the Trojans.
- I ended with the burning of the city of Troy.
- I spanned from around 1250 - 1240 BC.

THE TROJAN WAR

WHO AM I?

- I was made up of three wars.
- I was caused over jealousy between Sparta and Athens.
- I ended with the destruction of the Athenian Navy.
- I spanned from 431 - 404 BC.

THE PELOPONNESIAN WAR

WHO AM I?

- I am one of the most elaborate megalithic monument in Europe.
- It is thought I was built to mark midwinter's moon rise and midsummer's sunrise.
- I am located on the Salisbury Plain, England.
- I was finished around 2700 BC.

STONEHENGE

WHO AM I?

- My empire was the largest in the world.
- I conquered the Persians.
- I was the son of Philip II.
- I was 20 when I inherited the Macedon throne.
- I died at age 23.
- My life time was from 356 - 323 BC.

ALEXANDER THE GREAT

WHO AM I?

- I was widely read and memorized by the Greeks.
- I consisted of two poems.
- I was written by Homer who refined and rewrote many old stories and myths.
- I was composed around 700 BC.

THE ILIAD AND THE ODYSSEY

WHO AM I?

- I was known as the cruelest Roman Emperor.
- I was first to persecute the Christians.
- I had my mother and first wife murdered.
- It's rumored that I set Rome on fire and then blamed the Christians.
- I lived from 37 - 68.

NERO

WHO AM I?

- I was an event held to honor the gods.
- My participants were able to show off their athletic skills.
- I was held at the sanctuary of Zeus at Olympia, Greece.
- I was first held in 776 BC.

THE FIRST OLYMPICS

WHO AM I?

- I was known as the "Father of Modern Medicine."
- I used the power of observation to detect many different illnesses.
- I was born in Greece.
- I lived from around 460 - 377 BC.

HIPPOCRATES

WHO AM I?

- I was the first to insist that morality was part of philosophy.
- I was one of the world's greatest philosophers.
- I was the teacher of Plato.
- I lived from 469 - 399 BC.

SOCRATES

WHO AM I?

- I was made by a Roman Emperor.
- I was eventually changed by Pope Gregory XIII.
- I divided the year into twelve months.
- For three years I had 365 days and in the fourth I had 366 days.
- I was made around 45 BC.

THE JULIAN CALENDAR

WHO AM I?

- I wrote thirty or more works called "Dialogues."
- I believed that knowing the right questions is better than any particular set of answers.
- I was Socrates' most famous student.
- I lived from 427 - 347 BC.

PLATO

WHO AM I?

- I was first used by the Romans.
- I was used first in foundations.
- Eventually I was used in dome roofs.
- Now I am used in sidewalks and some highways.
- I was first used around 200 BC.

CONCRETE

WHO AM I?

- I recognized order, design, and purpose in the universe.
- I concluded that there had to be a single Supreme Being who gave order to the universe.
- I was Plato's most famous student.
- I lived from 384 - 322 BC.

ARISTOTLE

WHO AM I?

- I consisted of three wars.
- I was a war in which Athens and Sparta were allies.
- I was fought against Persia.
- The Greeks were victorious winning the first and third of my wars.
- I was fought from around 490 - 479 BC.

PERSIAN WARS

WHO AM I?

- I was one of the finest Greek temples.
- I was built with Ionic columns.
- I was located at the Acropolis in Athens.
- I was constructed from 477 - 432 BC.

THE PARTHENON

WHO AM I?

- I became king of Macedon at age 23.
- I immediately set about building the greatest army ever.
- By the time I died I controlled all of Greece.
- My son was Alexander the Great.
- I lived from 382 - 336 BC.

PHILIP II

WHO AM I?

- I consisted of three wars.
- I was fought between Carthage and Rome.
- I was fought over who would rule the Mediterranean world.
- Carthage was defeated in all three wars.
- I was fought between 264 - 146 BC.

PUNIC WARS

WHO AM I?

- I claimed to be a descendant of the gods.
- I conquered vast areas for Rome.
- I crossed the Rubicon River and took over Rome.
- I was murdered by Brutus who wanted to become emperor.
- I lived from 100 - 44 BC.

JULIUS CAESAR

WHO AM I?

- I was a general of Carthage during the Punic Wars, which we lost.
- I won three important battles for my country.
- I transported 50,000 men across the Alps with horses and elephants.
- I lived from 247 - 183 BC.

HANNIBAL

WHO AM I?

- I was close friends with Julius Caesar.
- Octavius and I divided up Julius' empire so we could both rule.
- I fell in love with Cleopatra.
- Thinking that she had killed herself, I did likewise.
- I lived from around 83 - 30 BC.

MARC ANTONY

WHO AM I?

- I was ruled by emperors.
- Most of my emperors died of unnatural causes.
- Huge roads connected every part of me.
- I made it possible for the word of God to spread around the world.
- I lasted from 31 BC - AD 476.

THE ROMAN EMPIRE

WHO AM I?

- I was the Roman emperor when Jesus was born.
- I started the Pax Romana.
- I defeated Marc Antony's navy.
- I extended the Roman empire to the Danube River.
- I lived from 63 BC - AD 14.

OCTAVIAN

WHO AM I?

- I was a Greek mathematician and inventor.
- I was born in Sicily.
- The Archimedes screw design was named after me.
- I lived from around 287 - 212 BC.

ARCHIMEDES

WHO AM I?

- I was the king of France.
- I was a very cruel king, once killing 4,500 rebels after they had surrendered.
- I spent nearly fifty years at war.
- I forced people to become Catholics wherever I conquered.
- I ruled from 771 - 814.

CHARLEMAGNE

WHO AM I?

- I was born in Venice and I took a trip with my father.
- I wrote a book about my journeys.
- I was only 17 when I went on my four year expedition.
- I brought spaghetti to Italy from China.
- I lived from 1254 - 1324.

MARCO POLO

 WHO AM I?

- I was given the command of three ships to explore the coast of Africa.
- Strong winds blew me off course and around the Cape of Good Hope.
- I drowned there near the Cape.
- I lived from around 1450 - 1500.

BARTHOLOMEU DIAS

  WHO AM I?

- I got my name for being so fierce.
- Sir Walter Scott wrote about my heroics.
- I participated in the Crusades.
- The king of the jungle is in my name.
- I lived from 1157 - 1199.

RICHARD THE LION HEARTED

 WHO AM I?

- I was born in Portugal.
- I believed I could get to India by sailing west.
- My trip was funded by the king and queen of Spain.
- I sailed west in three ships.
- I lived from 1451 - 1506.

CHRISTOPHER COLUMBUS

  WHO AM I?

- I was in a superman movie.
- I was built in Italy.
- I don't stand perfectly vertical.
- Part of my name sounds like "pizza."
- I was built in 1174.

THE LEANING TOWER OF PISA

 WHO AM I?

- I named the Pacific Ocean.
- I was credited with being the first to sail around the world.
- I died when we reached the Philippines.
- There is a strait in South America named after me.
- I lived from 1480 - 1521.

FERDINAND MAGELLAN

  WHO AM I?

- I was fought over land.
- I was fought between France and Britain.
- During me, the English used long bows and gun powder.
- I was eventually won by the French with the help of Joan of Arc.
- My time period is 1337 - 1453.

THE HUNDRED YEARS' WAR

 WHO AM I?

- I believed man was saved by faith alone, not by good works or indulgences.
- I started the Reformation.
- I nailed my Ninety-five Theses on the church door in Wittenberg.
- I lived from 1483 - 1546.

MARTIN LUTHER

WHO AM I?

- I was born to a wealthy family.
- I gave up all I had to help the sick and poor.
- I believed that a friar should work for a living and only beg when he could not work.
- After my death I was made a saint.
- I lived from 1182 - 1226.

ST. FRANCIS OF ASSISI

WHO AM I?

- My victims died within a couple of hours.
- I was spread by fleas first carried by rats and then by humans.
- I killed one-fourth the population of Europe and much of the Asian populations.
- I was a form of Bubonic Plague.
- I lasted from 1347 - 1353.

THE BLACK PLAGUE

WHO AM I?

- I was French, yet the English killed me.
- I was only a young girl, yet I encouraged many soldiers.
- I believed I was God's instrument.
- I helped the French win against the English in the Hundred Years' War.
- I lived from 1412 - 1431.

JOAN OF ARC

WHO AM I?

- I was invented by Roger Bacon.
- You could start fires with me.
- I made things appear larger.
- I was made in 1266.

THE MAGNIFYING GLASS

WHO AM I?

- I was a professor of theology.
- I denounced the wealth and corruption of the Church.
- I translated the Bible into English.
- I lived from around 1330 - 1384.

JOHN WYCLIFFE

WHO AM I?

- I wrote backward in my journals.
- I was an inventor, yet most of my ideas never worked while I was alive.
- People say I was born ahead of my time.
- I was also a great painter, artist, sculpturer, musician, architect, and engineer.
- I lived from 1452 - 1519.

LEONARDO DA VINCI

WHO AM I?

- I was first printed in England by William Caxton.
- Although a poem, I am full of political messages.
- The English poet Geoffrey Chaucer wrote me.
- I was written in 1388.

CANTERBURY TALES

WHO AM I?

- I was made up of the Eastern Roman Empire.
- My capital was Constantinople.
- I was the center of learning where Ancient Greek and the new Christian church were combined.
- I lasted from 395 - 1453.

THE BYZANTINE EMPIRE

WHO AM I?

- I went with my father to Greenland.
- I visited Newfoundland, yet my people and I never stayed.
- I was a Viking.
- My father was Eric the Red.
- I discovered North America in 1003.

LEIF ERICSSON

 ## WHO AM I?

- I fought at the Battle of Hastings.
- I was crowned king on Christmas day at Westminster Abbey.
- I was a Norman, crowned King of England.
- William of Normandy was my original name.
- I lived from 1027 - 1087.

WILLIAM THE CONQUEROR

 ## WHO AM I?

- I was started by the European nobles.
- I was thought to be a holy calling.
- I got out of hand and many people lost their lives for nothing.
- I was supposed to purify the Holy Land.
- I lasted from 1096 -1204.

THE CRUSADES

 ## WHO AM I?

- I divided the Frankish Empire into France and Germany.
- I was signed by King Louis' sons.
- I was a treaty.
- I was written up in 843.

TREATY OF VERDUN

 ## WHO AM I?

- I was an ambitious military leader.
- I combined the lands of Italy and Germany into one kingdom.
- My kingdom later became known as the Holy Roman Empire.
- I lived from 936 - 973.

OTTO I OF GERMANY

 ## WHO AM I?

- I was a document eventually used as the basis for freedom related documents.
- King John was forced, by his nobles, to sign me.
- I was considered a first step to self government.
- I was signed in 1215.

THE MAGNA CARTA

 ## WHO AM I?

- I was fought between the English and the Normans.
- I was also known as the Norman Invasion.
- The Normans won me.
- I was fought in 1066.

THE BATTLE OF HASTINGS

 ## WHO AM I?

- I was a special court established by Pope Gregory IX.
- My purpose was to purify the church of heretics.
- Those suspected of heresy were tried, tortured, imprisoned, and killed during me.
- I began in 1233.

THE INQUISITION

WHO AM I?

- My husband died 2 years after we married.
- I was a Catholic, but my home land was Protestant.
- I became Queen of Scotland when I was only one week old.
- I was executed in England.
- I lived from 1542 - 1587.

MARY QUEEN OF SCOTS

 WHO AM I?

- I was victorious over the four rival emperors fighting over the Roman Empire.
- I was the emperor that saw the cross and heard, "By this sign conquer."
- I was the first Roman Emperor to become a Christian.
- I lived from around 280 - 337.

CONSTANTINE

  WHO AM I?

- We married in 1469 to join two nations.
- We totally supported the Catholic Inquisition.
- Our army defeated the Moors and Jews.
- We supported Columbus in his exploration.
- Our time period was 1469 - 1516.

FERDINAND AND ISABELLA

WHO AM I?

- I was one of the greatest composers of my time.
- I was born in Germany.
- I wrote many pieces for the clavichord.
- My sons were also composers.
- I lived from 1685 - 1750.

JOHANN SEBASTIAN BACH

  WHO AM I?

- I was fought for religious reasons.
- I was fought between the Protestants and the Catholics.
- I ended with the Treaty of Westphalia.
- I lasted from 1618 - 1648.

THIRTY YEARS' WAR

WHO AM I?

- I was a poor student as a child but became a great scientist.
- I invented the reflecting telescope.
- I discovered three Laws of Motion.
- I wrote about the laws of gravity.
- I lived from 1642 - 1727.

ISAAC NEWTON

  WHO AM I?

- I was written when my author was in prison.
- I was an allegory.
- My author was John Bunyan.
- I was written in 1678.

A PILGRIM'S PROGRESS

WHO AM I?

- I was the movement that challenged the teachings of the Roman Catholic Church.
- The Protestant denomination began during me.
- I began when Martin Luther nailed his Ninety-five Theses on the church door.
- I started around 1516.

THE REFORMATION

WHO AM I?

- I was a famous painter and sculptor.
- I designed the dome of St. Peter's in Rome.
- I painted the Sistine Chapel.
- I lived from 1475 - 1564.

MICHELANGELO BUONARROTI

WHO AM I?

- The church thought my theories were contrary to the Bible.
- I believed the earth moved around the sun.
- I also believed the earth turned on its own axis.
- I lived from 1473 - 1543.

NICOLAUS COPERNICUS

WHO AM I?

- I was an actor in London.
- I was an Elizabethan playwright.
- I wrote plays, comedies, and tragedies.
- I lived from 1564 - 1616.

WILLIAM SHAKESPEARE

WHO AM I?

- I was a council called by Pope Paul III.
- I decided that nuns, monks, and priests should keep vows of poverty.
- I was known as the Counter Reformation.
- I was supposed to reform the Roman Catholic church.
- I was held in 1545.

COUNCIL OF TRENT

WHO AM I?

- I supported the Pope against Martin Luther.
- I had six different wives; I divorced two, executed two, one died naturally, and one outlived me.
- I started the Church of England.
- I ruled from 1509 - 1547.

HENRY VIII

WHO AM I?

- I set up the Protestant church in England.
- My fleet destroyed the Spanish Armada.
- I was the only child of Henry VIII and Anne Boleyn.
- I lived from 1558 - 1603.

QUEEN ELIZABETH

 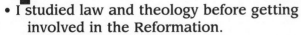

WHO AM I?

- I studied law and theology before getting involved in the Reformation.
- I was originally named John Chauvin.
- I believed in predestination and that only the elect would be saved.
- I started the Protestant Revolution.
- My time period is 1509 - 1564.

JOHN CALVIN

WHO AM I?

- I was born the same year as William Shakespeare and died the year Isaac Newton was born.
- I was the first to observe the stars through a telescope.
- I believed that the earth and the planets circled around the sun.
- I lived from 1564 - 1642.

GALILEO GALILEI

WHO AM I?

- I was fought for the power of Europe.
- I was fought between Britain and the Franks.
- I divided Europe into states.
- I ended when Tsar (Czar) Peter II came to power and called for peace.
- I lasted from 1756 - 1763.

THE SEVEN YEARS' WAR

 WHO AM I?

- I was born in Corsica.
- In 1799 I crowned myself emperor of France.
- By the age of 26 I was a general of the French army.
- My name was also the name of an ice-cream.
- I lived from 1769 - 1821.

NAPOLEON BONAPARTE

 WHO AM I?

- I was fought in France.
- I was started when a mob attacked a prison in Paris.
- The king, queen, and many nobility died during me.
- *The Scarlet Pimpernel* was set during me.
- I was fought from 1789 - 1799.

THE FRENCH REVOLUTION

 WHO AM I?

- I was an explorer.
- I was an artist, and I kept a journal of all I saw.
- I made three voyages to the Pacific region.
- I was killed in Hawaii.
- I lived from 1728 - 1779.

CAPTAIN JAMES COOK

 WHO AM I?

- I was held together with 2.5 million rivets.
- It took two years to build me.
- I stood 984 feet high.
- I was built for the Paris Exhibition.
- I was finished in 1889.

THE EIFFEL TOWER

 WHO AM I?

- I was fought between Germany and France.
- During me Germany defeated the French.
- Napoleon III lost his crown when he lost me.
- I lasted from 1870 - 1871.

FRANCO - PRUSSIAN WAR

 WHO AM I?

- I was a composer.
- I became deaf toward the end of my life.
- I was considered a bit eccentric.
- The Fifth Symphony was my most famous piece.
- I lived from 1770 - 1827.

LUDWIG VON BEETHOVEN

 WHO AM I?

- I was named for the area where I was fought.
- I was a rebellion which turned into a war.
- I was the end to the great Ottoman Empire.
- I lasted from 1829 - 1913.

THE BALKAN WARS

WHO AM I?

- I was a famous painter born in Spain.
- Some of my art shows the beginning of a new movement called Cubism.
- In my paintings, eyes and ears aren't always in the right place.
- I live from 1881 - 1973.

PABLO PICASSO

WHO AM I?

- I was fought between the Allies and the Central Powers.
- I was ended by the Treaty of Versailles.
- I was the "war to end all wars."
- I was fought from 1914 -1918.

WORLD WAR I

WHO AM I?

- I was one of two alliances.
- I was an agreement that if one of my parties were attacked the others would come to their rescue.
- My participants were Germany, Austria, Hungry, and Italy.
- I lasted from 1882 - 1915.

THE TRIPLE ALLIANCE

WHO AM I?

- I was one of the largest oceanliners of my time.
- Over 1,000 people died when German U-boats sank me.
- My sinking contributed to the United States entering WWI.
- I sank in 1915.

THE LUSITANIA

WHO AM I?

- I was one of two alliances.
- Because of me, if someone went to war with one of my participants, the others supported them.
- My participants were Great Britain, France, and Russia.
- I lasted from 1890 - 1915.

THE TRIPLE ENTENTE

WHO AM I?

- I was the treaty that ended WWI.
- Because of me, Germany had to give up Alsace-Lorraine overseas colonies and all lands they took by force.
- I also strictly limited Germany's armed forces.
- I was signed in 1919.

TREATY OF VERSAILLES

WHO AM I?

- I was an Arch Duke.
- I was the heir to the Austro-Hungarian throne.
- My assassination was the spark that triggered WWI.
- I died in 1914.

FRANCIS FERDINAND

WHO AM I?

- I was born in Austria.
- I served in the German army during WWI and even won the Iron Cross.
- I became the socialist leader of Germany and started WWII with my actions.
- I lived from 1889 - 1945.

ADOLF HITLER

WHO AM I?

- I was born in Italy.
- I was kicked out of the Socialist party because of my role in WWI.
- I became the dictator of Italy and entered WWII on the Axis side.
- I lived from 1883 - 1945.

BENITO MUSSOLINI

WHO AM I?

- I was the invasion of Normandy by the Allies.
- The Germans had a counter attack during me but they had to retreat.
- I began the end of the Nazis - reign of terror.
- I happened in 1944.

D - DAY

WHO AM I?

- I was a war fought in Spain.
- I was started over the question of political leaders.
- Francisco Franco was a great military leader during me.
- I was fought from 1936 - 1939.

THE SPANISH CIVIL WAR

WHO AM I?

- I founded the Methodist Church.
- I was one of the most famous men in English history.
- I led Europe in revival.
- I was one of nineteen children born to my mother, Susanna Wesley.
- I lived from 1703 - 1791.

JOHN WESLEY

WHO AM I?

- I was fought between the Allies and the Axis.
- I pulled the U.S. out of their Great Depression.
- The U.S. entered me when the Japanese bombed Pearl Harbor.
- I was fought from 1939 - 1945.

WORLD WAR II

WHO AM I?

- I was the leader of the Irish Citizen Army.
- I founded the Irish Socialist Republican Party in 1896.
- I was shot while in jail because of being involved in the Easter Rising.
- I lived from 1870 - 1916.

JAMES CONNOLLY

WHO AM I?

- I was signed by Hitler, Mussolini, Neville Chamberlain, and Edouard Daladier.
- Britain and France mistakenly believed I would keep Europe at peace.
- I established new boundaries in Europe after WWI.
- I was signed in 1938.

MUNICH AGREEMENT

WHO AM I?

- My verdict convicted many innocent people to hang on the gallows.
- It is believed that I began because of religious superstition.
- *The Crucible* was written about me.
- I occurred in 1692.

SALEM WITCH TRIALS

Who Am I?

- I occurred because of taxation without representation.
- 340 tea crates were destroyed and dumped into the harbor during me.
- My participants were patriots dressed up as Indians.
- I occurred in 1773.

The Boston Tea Party

Who Am I?

- I attracted people from all over the world.
- A man by the name of James Marshall found the first gold that started me.
- Because of me gold seekers were called forty-niners.
- Not all miners struck it rich during me.
- I started in 1849.

The California Gold Rush

Who Am I?

- I was fought for freedom.
- I was started by "The Shot Heard 'Round the World."
- My participants were nicknamed the Yankees and the Redcoats.
- I lasted from 1776 - 1783.

American War For Independence (Revolutionary War)

Who Am I?

- I was known as "The Liberator."
- I led many victories over the Spaniards.
- I won the independence of Bolivia, Colombia, Ecuador, Peru, and Venezuela.
- I was from a wealthy family in Venezuela.
- I lived from 1783 - 1830.

Simon Bolivar

Who Am I?

- I acknowledged that God created all men equal and they have certain rights that cannot be taken away.
- I was written by a committee led by Thomas Jefferson.
- There's a holiday in my honor that is celebrated by Americans.
- My time period is 1776.

The Declaration of Independence

Who Am I?

- A president was assassinated because of me.
- When I ended, over 5,000 men had died and 18,000 were wounded.
- My first battle took place at Fort Sumter.
- The surrender at Appomattox ended me.
- I was fought from 1861 - 1865.

American Civil War

Who Am I?

- I ended the American War for Independence.
- By me the King of England recognized the thirteen colonies as independent.
- I was signed between the U.S.A. and England.
- I was signed in 1783.

Treaty Of Paris

Who Am I?

- I was a German Jew who moved to America and became a U.S. citizen.
- I was a physicist who was once kicked out of school because I was thought to be stupid.
- My research on atoms helped develop the worst weapon in the world at that time.
- I lived from 1879 - 1955.

Albert Einstein

WHO AM I?

- I invented the assembly line.
- I wanted to build an automobile that the average American could afford.
- My most famous invention was the Model-T.
- I lived from 1863 - 1947.

HENRY FORD

WHO AM I?

- When I was first released I captivated people.
- Although common today, I was a technical marvel in my day.
- Many people would spend hours daily watching me.
- I was invented in 1950.

THE COLOR TV

WHO AM I?

- I helped Rosa Parks set up an organization to boycott the city bus system.
- I helped form the Southern Christian Leadership Conference (SCLC).
- I was shot and killed because of my beliefs and skin color.
- I lived from 1929 - 1968.

MARTIN LUTHER KING JR.

WHO AM I?

- When I was first invented I entertained people at night.
- Once, a program was played that terrified many people.
- People gathered around me to hear the latest news of war.
- My first broadcast in the USA was in 1920.

RADIO

WHO AM I?

- I was an event that had millions glued to their radios and TVs.
- I was the culmination of the "Space Race."
- I was accomplished by the Apollo 11 astronauts.
- I occurred in 1969.

MAN WALKS ON MOON

WHO AM I?

- I stand 120 feet high.
- I weigh 204 tons.
- I was a gift to the U.S.A. from France.
- I greeted immigrants to the United States.
- I was finished in 1886.

THE STATUE OF LIBERTY

WHO AM I?

- The Hay-Pauncefote Treaty made it possible for my construction.
- I was located in Central America.
- I am fifty miles long and consist of many locks and dams.
- I was finished in 1914.

PANAMA CANAL

WHO AM I?

- My towers were the first things ships saw as they reached the coast of California.
- I was one of the largest suspension bridges in the world.
- I spann 6,450 feet to connect California to the peninsula of San Francisco.
- I was built in 1937.

GOLDEN GATE BRIDGE

44

WHO AM I?

- I was a fortified mission near San Antonio.
- Davy Crockett fought at me.
- At me, 187 Americans held off General Santa Anna's army for almost two weeks.
- I was defended by the Americans in 1836.

THE ALAMO

WHO AM I?

- I claimed the land that is now known as New York for Holland.
- I sailed my ship, the Half Moon, into the Delaware Bay and the Hudson River.
- That river bears my name.
- I died in 1611.

HENRY HUDSON

WHO AM I?

- I established the Bureau of Missing Persons during the Civil War.
- Wounded soldiers called me the "Angel of the Battlefield."
- I started the American Red Cross.
- I lived from 1821 - 1912.

CLARA BARTON

WHO AM I?

- I was a Cherokee Indian.
- I invented the only written language for the North American tribes.
- The giant redwoods in California were named after me.
- I lived from 1770 - 1843.

SEQUOYAH

WHO AM I?

- I enabled 1 person to process fifty pounds of cotton a day compared to one pound.
- I increased cotton plantation productivity in the 19th century.
- I was invented by Eli Whitney.
- I was made in 1793.

THE COTTON GIN

WHO AM I?

- I was based on the idea that government should assume more responsibility.
- Because of me the U.S. government has many different programs to benefit the welfare of the people.
- I was FDR's political program.
- I was started from 1933 - 1945.

THE NEW DEAL

WHO AM I?

- I was a law that opened the great plains of the west for settlement.
- I granted 160 acres to anyone who would be willing to farm and live on the land.
- Many new settlers established communities in the west because of me.
- I went into effect in 1862.

THE HOMESTEAD ACT

WHO AM I?

- Many movies have been made about me.
- I was supposed to be unsinkable.
- I sank on my maiden voyage after I hit an iceberg.
- I disappeared in to the depths of the ocean in 1912.

THE TITANIC

4 5

WHO AM I?

- We explored the West for President Thomas Jefferson.
- We took an eighteen month exploration to the Pacific Ocean.
- One of us kept a detailed journal of all we found or saw.
- Our expedition lasted from 1804 - 1806.

THE LEWIS AND CLARK EXPEDITION

WHO AM I?

- I was a document that warned against the further colonization of the Americas by Europe.
- Any infraction of me would be considered an unfriendly act.
- I was issued by President Monroe.
- I went into effect in 1823.

MONROE DOCTRINE

WHO AM I?

- I am an inventor.
- My wife tapped Morse Code on my leg so I could understand plays and orations because I couldn't hear.
- I invented the light bulb, phonograph, kinescope and over 1000 other things.
- I lived from 1847 - 1931.

THOMAS EDISON

WHO AM I?

- I started at St. Joseph, Missouri, and went to San Francisco.
- I could reach my destination in ten days.
- I was the fastest mail service in the mid 19th century.
- The start of the transcontinental railroad ended my usefulness.
- I lasted from 1860 - 1861.

THE PONY EXPRESS

WHO AM I?

- I was born into a noble Spanish family.
- I grew up in the West Indies.
- I conquered the Aztecs.
- I lived from 1485 - 1547.

HERNAN CORTES

WHO AM I?

- I carried two-thirds of the U.S. internal trade.
- I was started by two different companies on opposite sides of the U.S.
- A Golden Spike marked my completion.
- I was the first railroad to cross the U.S.
- I was opened in 1869.

THE TRANSCONTINENTAL RAILROAD

WHO AM I?

- I was founded by William Booth.
- I was established to help the poor improve their lives.
- I am still active today.
- I started in 1865.

THE SALVATION ARMY

WHO AM I?

- I educated the black community and taught them to live without government aid.
- I fought for better education for my black brothers.
- I founded Tuskegee Institute in Alabama.
- I lived from 1856 - 1915.

BOOKER T. WASHINGTON

WHO AM I?

- I was born in Spain.
- I took part in the Spanish Conquest of Central America when I was 19.
- I was the first white man to cross the Mississippi River.
- I lived from 1500 - 1542.

HERNANDO DE SOTO

WHO AM I?

- My rise to power made the world fear me.
- The prophet Isaiah is said to have written about me hundreds of years before I was born.
- I was the Persian king who was victorious over the Medes.
- I died around 529 BC.

CYRUS OF PERSIA

WHO AM I?

- I was written before the U.S. Constitution.
- I allowed the creation of new states north and west of the Ohio River.
- I guaranteed trial by jury, public education, freedom of religion, and prohibited slavery.
- I was written in 1787.

NORTHWEST ORDINANCE

WHO AM I?

- I was one of the ancient Seven Wonders of the World.
- I was located in the Babylonian Empire.
- I was built by King Nebuchadnezzar for his wife.
- I was build in 580 BC.

THE HANGING GARDENS

WHO AM I?

- I am used by almost everyone in the world today.
- I made communication very easy.
- I was invented by Alexander Graham Bell.
- I was designed in 1875.

THE TELEPHONE

WHO AM I?

- Orkhan was my first ruler.
- I was founded shortly after the Crusades.
- I was located in and around Turkey.
- I lasted from 1300 - 1918.

OTTOMAN EMPIRE

WHO AM I?

- I was a king of Babylon.
- I was a master of what is known today as "Machiavellian politics."
- I was chiefly known because of my code of laws.
- I reigned from 1792 - 1750 BC.

HAMMURABI

WHO AM I?

- My name meant "highly praised."
- I was born in Mecca.
- I was convinced I was the appointed prophet of Allah.
- I established the Muslim or Islam religion.
- I lived from 570 - 631.

MOHAMMED (MUHAMMAD)

4 7

WHO AM I?

- We could be compared to the knights of the Middle Ages.
- We would be willing to fight to the death for our daimyos (overlords).
- We were the warrior class in China.
- We were from around 1000 - 1877.

SAMURAI

 WHO AM I?

- For eighteen months I observed Europe's industry bringing information to Russia.
- I jerked backward Russia into a mighty European power.
- In a war with Sweden I obtained Estonia and Livonia.
- I ruled from 1689 - 1725.

PETER THE GREAT, CZAR OF RUSSIA

   WHO AM I?

- I changed my name from Temujin when I was 39 years old.
- I conquered northern China and overran Afghanistan, Persia, and Turkestan.
- I became leader of my tribe at age 13 when my father was poisoned.
- In some ways my empire was greater than Alexander the Great's.
- I lived from 1167 - 1227.

GENGHIS KHAN

 WHO AM I?

- Babur founded me when he invaded India from Afghanistan.
- I covered most of India at one point.
- The Taj Mahal was built during me.
- I lasted from 1527 - 1803.

MONGUL EMPIRE

   WHO AM I?

- My name means "brightness."
- My first ruler was Hung Wu.
- My emperors were great builders.
- My period is known for my blue and white porcelain.
- I lasted from 1368 - 1644.

MING DYNASTY

 WHO AM I?

- I was the first war in which the public was kept informed by photographs and reports.
- I was a struggle over territory because of the collapse of the Ottoman Empire.
- Florence Nightingale was a nurse during me.
- I lasted from 1854 - 1856.

THE CRIMEAN WAR

   WHO AM I?

- I was located in Agra, India.
- I was built with white marble inlaid with detailed patterns of semi-precious stones.
- I was built for the Mongul ruler, Shah Jahan's favorite wife.
- It took twenty-one years to complete me.
- I was built between 1629 - 1650.

THE TAJ MAHAL

 WHO AM I?

- I was started because Russia expanded into Manchuria.
- I was between the Russians and the Japanese.
- At the Battle of Tsushima the Russians were defeated.
- I lasted from 1904 - 1905.

THE RUSSO - JAPANESE WAR

WHO AM I?

- I was born in India yet studied law in England.
- When I went back to India I was jailed many times because of my campaigns.
- My philosophy of nonviolence made me popular and unpopular at the same time.
- I lived from 1869 - 1948.

MAHATMA GANDHI

WHO AM I?

- I was born during the Chou dynasty.
- I was also known as K'ung Fu-tzu.
- I taught morality and responsibility.
- I influenced Chinese thought.
- I lived from 551 - 479 BC.

CONFUCIUS

WHO AM I?

- I was invented by Han scientists.
- I have a dial and a pointer.
- I was first used to make sure temples were facing the right direction.
- I was later used for navigation.
- I was invented around 270.

MAGNETIC COMPASS

WHO AM I?

- I was 23 feet wide.
- I was constructed of rubble covered by bricks and stone.
- I originally stretched 1,400 miles, but if you add all my curves I was over 4,000 miles long.
- I was built between 218 - 204 BC.

THE GREAT WALL OF CHINA

WHO AM I?

- During me metalworkers made bronze.
- I was the first known Chinese dynasty.
- My people were mostly farmers.
- I lasted from 1500 - 1122 BC.

SHANG DYNASTY

WHO AM I?

- China gets its name from me.
- Shi Huangdi was the first emperor during me.
- A single type of money was introduced during me.
- I lasted from 221 - 207 BC.

CHI'N (QIN) DYNASTY

WHO AM I?

- My people were wandering herders..
- During me iron was introduced to use in tools.
- I had a collection of large estates whose owners were loyal to the king.
- My time period is 1122 - 256 BC.

CHOU (ZHOU) DYNASTY

WHO AM I?

- I was founded by Li Yuan.
- Gun powder was invented during me.
- The silk trade grew and flourished during me.
- I lasted from 618 - 907.

TANG DYNASTY (AGE OF TANG)

WHO AM I?

- I was born in Russia.
- I became a Marxist after my brother was killed for attempting to assassinate the Tzar.
- I formed the USSR.
- I lived from 1870 - 1924.

VLADIMIR LENIN

 WHO AM I?

- I united Upper and Lower Egypt.
- I was the first Pharaoh of all Egypt.
- I started the rules of the dynasties in Egypt.
- My rule started around 3000 BC.

PHARAOH MENES

 WHO AM I?

- I happened during WW I.
- I caused Russia to pull out of WWI.
- During me the Tzar and his family were executed.
- I occurred in 1917.

THE BOLSHEVIK REVOLUTION

 WHO AM I?

- We were built by Pharaoh Khufu during the Old Kingdom.
- We are located at Giza.
- One of us housed the dead pharaohs and their wealth.
- The other is part man part lion.
- We were built around 2551 BC.

THE SPHINX AND THE GREAT PYRAMIDS

 WHO AM I?

- I was a series of wars fought between the British and China.
- At the end of me China had to give up Hong Kong and open many ports.
- I caused the breakdown of the mighty Chinese Empire.
- I lasted from 1839 - 1860.

OPIUM WARS

 WHO AM I?

- The most famous of us was King Tut.
- If I were a pharaoh, I would be placed in a pyramid or tomb.
- I was the result of a process in which the dead were preserved.
- I was first used in 2500 BC.

MUMMIES

  WHO AM I?

- I was well known for my beauty and my intelligence.
- I charmed the great men of Rome.
- I was known as "Queen of the Nile."
- I reigned from 69 - 30 BC.

CLEOPATRA

 WHO AM I?

- I was the time period in Egypt of the 4th to the 8th dynasties.
- Zoser was my first Pharaoh.
- The great Pyramids and the Sphinx were built during me.
- I lasted from 2575 - 2134 BC.

THE OLD KINGDOM

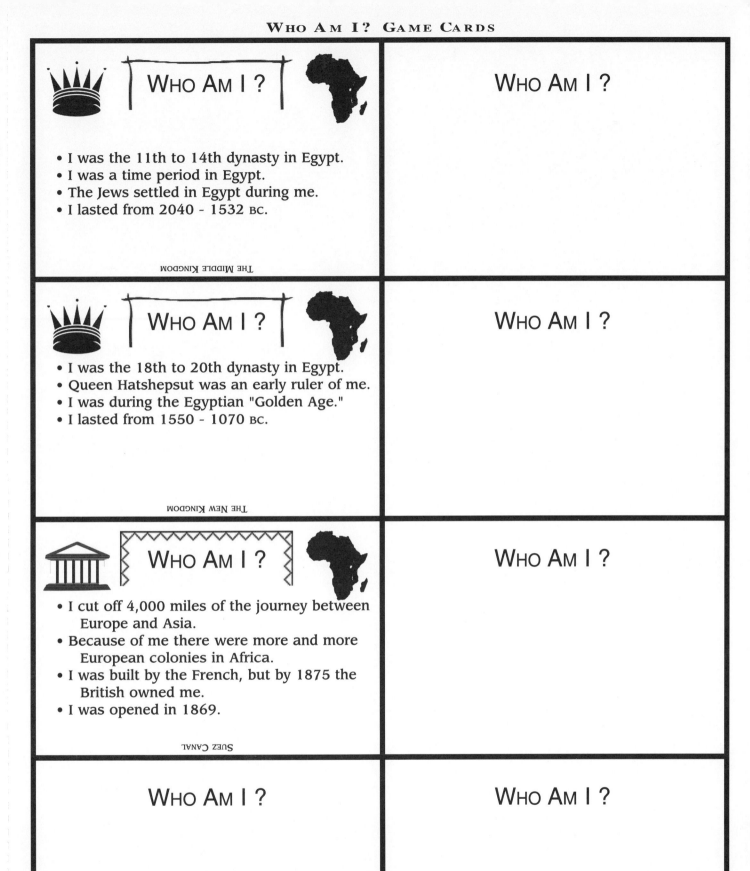

WHO AM I?

- I was the 11th to 14th dynasty in Egypt.
- I was a time period in Egypt.
- The Jews settled in Egypt during me.
- I lasted from 2040 - 1532 BC.

THE MIDDLE KINGDOM

WHO AM I?

WHO AM I?

- I was the 18th to 20th dynasty in Egypt.
- Queen Hatshepsut was an early ruler of me.
- I was during the Egyptian "Golden Age."
- I lasted from 1550 - 1070 BC.

THE NEW KINGDOM

WHO AM I?

WHO AM I?

- I cut off 4,000 miles of the journey between Europe and Asia.
- Because of me there were more and more European colonies in Africa.
- I was built by the French, but by 1875 the British owned me.
- I was opened in 1869.

SUEZ CANAL

WHO AM I?

WHO AM I?

WHO AM I?

Chronological List of Dates

c 3800 BC	Earliest Known Map
c 3760 BC	Bronze First Used
3372 BC	First Day in Mayan Calendar
c 3200 BC	Writing Appears
3000 BC	Wheeled Vehicles
c 3000 BC	First Iron Objects Made
c 3000 BC	Pharaoh Menes
2700 BC	Stonehenge
c 2600 BC	Papyrus Used as Paper
2773 BC	Calendar with 365 Days
c 2690 BC	Chinese Start Weaving Silk
2575-2134 BC	Old Kingdom (Egypt)
c 2686-2181 BC	Age of Pyramids
2551 BC	Sphinx & Great Pyramids Built
2500 BC	First Mummies
2500 BC	First Surgery (Egypt)
2040-1532 BC	Middle Kingdom (Egypt)
c 2000 BC	Basis for Modern Alphabet
2000 BC	China's First Zoo
1792-1750 BC	Hammurabi's Reign
1500 BC	Glass Bottles Used (Egypt)
1550-1070 BC	New Kingdom (Egypt)
1500-1122 BC	Shang Dynasty
c 1250-1240 BC	Trojan War
1100-900 BC	First Chinese Language Dictionary
1122-256 BC	Chou (Zhou) Dynasty
776 BC	First Olympic Games
755 BC	First Date in Chinese History
722 BC	N. Kingdom of Israel Destroyed
700 BC	First Coins Used
c 700 BC	Iliad & Odyssey
600 BC	Windmills Used
580 BC	The Hanging Gardens
580?-497 BC	Pythagoras
563-483 BC	Buddha
551-479 BC	Confucius
539 BC	Fall of Babylon
?-529 BC	Cyrus of Persia
508 BC	Athens 1st Democracy
c 490-479 BC	Persian War
480 BC	Greek Classical Period
477-432 BC	Parthenon
477-405 BC	Golden Age of Athens
469-399 BC	Socrates
460 BC	Parchment Replaces Stone Tablets
c 460-377 BC	Hippocrates
431-404 BC	Peloponnesian War
427-347 BC	Plato
390 BC	First Kite
384-322 BC	Aristotle
382-336 BC	Philip II
356-323 BC	Alexander the Great
323-319 BC	Alexander's Empire Divided
c 287-212 BC	Archimedes
264-146 BC	Punic War
247-183 BC	Hannibal
221-207 BC	Chin (Qin) Dynasty
218-204 BC	Great Wall of China
c 206 BC-AD 221	Han Dynasty
c 200 BC	Concrete First Used (Rome)
c 150 BC	Silk Paintings / Pottery Fig.
100-44 BC	Julius Caesar
c 83-30 BC	Marc Antony
69-30 BC	Cleopatra's Reign
63 BC-AD 14	Octavian (Caesar Augusts)
50 BC-AD 50	Buddhism Introduced
c 45 BC	Julian Calendar
31 BC-AD 476	Roman Empire
c 4	Birth of Jesus
42	The First Pope
54-68	First Persecution
37-68	Nero
64	Rome Destroyed by Fire
90-168	Ptolemy
100	Ethiopia Wealthy
c 270	Magnetic Compass
c 280-337	Constantine
300-600	Mayan Golden Age
320-535	Great Gupta Empire
395	Roman Empire Divided
395-1453	Byzantine Empire
476	Last Roman Emperor Dethroned
c 503	Legendary King Arthur
570-631	Mohammed (Muhammad)
593	Wooden Blocks Used for Printing (China)
605-610	Imperial Canal Built
618-907	T'ang Dynasty
622	Islam Introduced
771-841	Charlemagne
843	Treaty of Verdun
847	Vikings Settle Iceland
858-867	Pope Nicholas I
900	Age of Iron & Steel
932	First Mass Production of Books
960-1279	Song Dynasty
936-973	Otto I of Germany
962-1806	The New Holy Roman Empire
c 1000-c 1877	Samurai
1003	Leif Ericsson Discovers North America

1027-1087	William the Conqueror	1590	Microscope Invented
1054	Catholic Church Divides	1598	Henry IV Converts to Catholicism
1056-1147	Almorarid Kingdom	1607	Virginia Colony Founded
1066	The Battle of Hastings	?-1611	Henry Hudson
1077	Pope George VII Challenges Henry IV	1610	Galileo's Telescope
1096-1204	The Crusades	1611	King James Bible
1099	Jerusalem Falls to Crusaders	1618-1648	The Thirty Years' War
c 1150	Paper First Made (Europe)	1620	Pilgrims Reach Cape Cod
1157-1199	Richard the Lion Hearted	1626	Madagascar Settled by French
1174	Leaning Tower of Pisa	1629-1650	Taj Mahal Built
1182-1226	St. Francis of Assisi	1636	First College, Harvard
1167-1227	Genghis Khan	1638-1715	Louis XIV of France
1215	Magna Carta Signed	1640	Puritan Revolution, England
1232	Rockets Used in Battle	1642-1648	English Civil War
1233	The Inquisition Begins	1642-1727	Isaac Newton
1254-1324	Marco Polo	1644-1912	Manchu Dynasty
1266	Magnifying Glass	1666	The Great Fire of London
1279-1368	Mongol Empire	1678	Pilgrim's Progress
c 1300-1918	Ottoman Empire	1682	Quakers Settle Pennsylvania
1309-1377	The Popes Dominated by French	1685-1750	Johann Sebastian Bach
c 1330-1384	John Wycliffe	1689-1725	Peter the Great
1325	Tenochtitlan Founded	1692	Salem Witch Trials
1337-1453	Hundred Years' War	1703-1791	John Wesley
1347-1353	Black Plague	1728-1779	Captain James Cook
1368-1644	Ming Dynasty	1756-1763	Seven Years' War
1380	Bible Now in English	1769-1821	Napoleon Bonaparte
1388	Canterbury Tales	1770-1827	Ludwig Von Beethoven
1412-1431	Joan of Arc	1770-1843	Sequoya
1440	Movable Type Used (Europe)	1773	Boston Tea Party
c 1450-1500	Bartholomeu Dias	1776	Declaration of Independence
1451-1506	Christopher Columbus	1776-1783	Revolutionary War
1452-1519	Leonardo da Vinci	1783	Treaty of Paris
1455-1485	War of the Roses	1783-1830	Simon Bolivar
1460-1521	Ponce de Leon	1787	Northwest Ordinance
1469-1516	Ferdinand & Isabella	1789-1797	George Washington
1473-1543	Nicolaus Copernicus	1789-1799	The French Revolution
1475-1564	Michelangelo Buonaroti	1793	Cotton Gin
1478	Spain Established	1797-1801	John Adams
1478	Spanish Inquisition	1801-1809	Thomas Jefferson
1480-1521	Ferdinand Magellan	1803	Louisiana Purchase
1483-1546	Martin Luther	1804-1806	Lewis & Clark Expedition
1485-1547	Hernan Cortes	1809-1817	James Madison
1492	Modern Globe	1817-1825	James Monroe
c 1494-1536	William Tyndale	1818-1883	Karl Marx
1500-1542	Hernando de Soto	1820-1910	Florence Nightingale
1502	African Slaves in America	1821-1912	Clara Barton
1504	First Watch	1823	Monroe Doctrine
1509-1564	John Calvin	1825-1829	John Quincy Adams
1509-1547	Henry VIII	1829	Greece Independence
c 1516	The Reformation Starts	1829-1837	Andrew Jackson
1527-1803	Mongul Empire	1829-1913	Balkan Wars
1528	First Surgery (Europe)	1836	The Alamo
1529	Henry VIII Separates from the Church	1837-1841	Martin Van Buren
1542-1587	Mary Queen of Scots	1839-1860	Opium War
1543	Scientific Revolution	1841	William Harrison
1545	Council of Trent	1841-1845	John Tyler
c 1552-1618	Sir Walter Raleigh	1844	YMCA Founded
1558-1603	Queen Elizabeth	1845-1849	James Polk
1564-1616	William Shakespeare	1846-1848	U.S. War with Mexico
1564-1642	Galileo Galilei	1847-1931	Thomas Edison
1587	Holland's Independence	1849	California Gold Rush
1588	Spanish Armada Defeated	1849-1850	Zachary Taylor

53

1850-1853	Millard Fillmore
1853-1857	Franklin Pierce
1854-1856	Crimean War
1856-1915	Booker T. Washington
1857-1861	James Buchanan
1860-1861	Pony Express
1861-1865	Abraham Lincoln
1861-1865	Civil War
1862-1908	Empress Tzu Hui
1862	Homestead Act
1863-1947	Henry Ford
1865	The Salvation Army
1865-1869	Andrew Jonson
1869	Suez Canal Opened
1869	Transcontinental Railroad
1869-1877	Ulysses Grant
1869-1948	Mahatma Gandhi
1870-1871	Franko-Prussian War
1870-1916	James Connoly
1870-1924	Vladimir Lenin
1877-1881	Rutherford Hayes
1875	The Telephone
1879-1955	Albert Einstein
1881	James Garfield
1881-1885	Chester Arthur
1881-1973	Pablo Picasso
1882-1915	The Triple Alliance
1883-1945	Benito Mussolini
1885-1889	Grover Cleveland
1886	Statue of Liberty
1889	Eiffel Tower
1889-1893	Benjamin Harrison
1889-1945	Adolf Hitler
1890-1915	The Triple Entente
1893-1897	Grover Cleveland
1897-1901	William McKinley
1901-1909	Theodore Roosevelt
1903	Airplane Invented
1904-1905	Russo-Japanese War
1909	First Resettlement of Israel
1909-1913	William Taft
1912	The Titanic Sinks
1913-1921	Woodrow Wilson
?-1914	Francis Ferdinand
1914	Panama Canal Finished
1914	First Traffic Lights
1914-1918	World War I
1915	The Lusitania Sinks
1915	Poison Gas Used in War
1916	Tanks Used in Battle
1917	Bolshevik Revolution
1919	The League of Nations
1919	Prohibition
1919	Treaty of Versailles
1920	Radio Broadcasting in U.S.
1921-1923	Warren Harding
1922	Egypt's Independence from Britain
1923-1929	Calvin Coolidge
1924	Indians Become American Citizens
1928	First Mickey Mouse Cartoon
1929	U.S. Stock Market Crashes
1929-1932	The Great Depression

1929-1933	Herbert Hoover
1929-1968	Martin Luther King Jr.
1933-1945	Franklin Roosevelt
1933-1945	The New Deal
1936-1939	Spanish Civil War
1937	Golden Gate Bridge
1938	Munich Agreement
1939-1945	World War II
1940	Miracle of Dunkirk
1941	Japanese Attack Pearl Harbor
1944	D-Day
1945	Atom Bomb First Used
1945-1953	Harry Truman
1946	People's Republic of China
1949	The Apartheid Policy
1949	NATO
1950	Color TV
1953-1961	Dwight Eisenhower
1954	Polio Vaccination
1961-1963	John Kennedy
1962	Prayer Removed from Schools
1962	Algeria's Independence from France
1963-1969	Lyndon Johnson
1969	Man Walks on Moon
1969-1974	Richard Nixon
1973	Abortion Legalized
1974-1977	Gerald Ford
1977-1981	Jimmy Carter
1981	First Space Shuttle
1981-1989	Ronald Reagan
1987	The Channel Tunnel
1989-1993	George Bush
1991	Commonwealth of Independent States
1991	Persian Gulf War
1993-?	William Clinton

Index

A

Abortion Legalized	15
Adams, John	17
Adams, John Quincy	17
African Slaves in America	14
Age of Iron & Steel	12
Age of Pyramids	11
Airplane Invented	14
Alamo	16, 45
Alexander's Empire Divided	22
Alexander the Great	22, 32
Algeria's Independence from France	11
Almorarid Kingdom	11
Antony, Marc	20, 34
Apartheid Policy	11
Archimedes	20, 34
Aristotle	22, 33
Arthur, Chester	17
Athens 1st Democracy	20
Atom Bomb First Used	16

B

Babylon Falls	26
Bach, Johann Sebastian	21, 38
Balkan Wars	25, 40
Barton, Clara	16, 45
Basis for Modern Alphabet	26
Battle of Hastings	24, 37
Beethoven, Ludwig Von	25, 40
Bible Now in English	19
Black Plague	19, 36
Bolivar, Simon	16, 43
Bolshevik Revolution	13, 50
Bonaparte, Napoleon	25, 40
Boston Tea Party	14, 43
Bronze First Used	26
Buchanan, James	17
Buddha	12
Buddhism Introduced (China)	12
Buonarroti, Michelangelo	23, 39
Bush, George	18
Byzantine Empire	19, 36

C

Caesar Augustus	22
Caesar, Julius	22, 34
Calendar with 365 Days	11
California Gold Rush	14, 43
Calvin, John	20, 39
Canterbury Tales	19, 36
Carter, James	18
Catholic Church Divides	24
Charlemagne	24, 34
China's First Zoo	12
Chin (Qin) Dynasty	12, 49
Chinese History, First Date	12
Chinese Language Dictionary	12
Chinese Start Weaving Silk	12
Chou Dynasty	12, 49
"Chunnel"	21
Civil War	14, 43
Cleopatra's Reign	11, 50

Cleveland, Grover	18
Clinton, William	18
Coins First Used	11
Color TV	16, 44
Columbus, Christopher	23, 35
Commonwealth of Independent States (CIS)	21
Concrete First Used	22, 33
Confucius	13, 49
Connoly, James	19, 42
Constantine	20, 38
Cook, James	25, 40
Coolidge, Calvin	18
Copernicus, Nicolaus	20, 39
Cortes, Hernan	14, 46
Cotton Gin	15, 45
Council of Trent	23, 39
Crimean War	13, 48
Crusades	24, 37
Cyrus of Persia	26, 47

D

da Vinci, Leonardo	19, 36
D-Day	24, 42
Declaration of Independence	14, 43
de Leon, Ponce	23
de Soto, Hernando	14, 47
Dias, Bartholomeu	23, 35

E

Earliest Known Map	26
Edison, Thomas	14, 46
Egypt's Independence from Britain	11
Eiffel Tower	25, 40
Einstein, Albert	16, 43
Eisenhower, Dwight	18
Empress Tzu Hui	13
English Civil War	21
Ethiopia Wealthy	11

F

Ferdinand & Isabella	23, 38
Ferdinand, Francis	24, 41
Fillmore, Millard	17
Ford, Gerald	18
Ford, Henry	16, 44
Franko-Prussian War	25, 40
French Revolution	25, 40

G

Galileo Galilei	23, 39
Galileo's Telescope	21
Gandhi, Mahatma	13, 49
Garfield, James	17
Glass Bottles First Used	11
Golden Age of Athens	22
Golden Gate Bridge	16, 44
Grant, Ulysses	17
Great Depression	16
Great Fire of London	21
Great Gupta Empire	12
Great Wall of China	12, 49

Greek Classical Period	22
Greek Independence	25

H

Hammurabi's Reign	26, 47
Han Dynasty	12
Hanging Gardens	26, 47
Hannibal	22, 34
Harding, Warren	18
Harrison, Benjamin	18
Harrison, William	17
Harvard College	15
Hayes, Rutherford	17
Henry IV Converts to Catholicism	23
Henry VIII	23, 39
Henry VIII Separates from the Church	23
Hippocrates	20, 32
Hitler, Adolf	25, 41
Holland's Independence	23
Homestead Act	15, 45
Hoover, Herbert	18
Hudson, Henry	15, 45
Hundred Years' War	19, 35

I

Iliad & Odyssey	20, 32
Imperial Canal Built	12
Indians Become American Citizens	15
Inquisition Begins	19, 37
Iron Objects First Made	26
Islam Introduced	26

J

Jackson, Andrew	17
Japanese Attack Pearl Harbor	14
Jefferson, Thomas	17
Jesus's Birth	26
Joan of Arc	19, 36
Johnson, Andrew	17
Johnson, Lyndon	18
Julian Calendar	22, 33
Jerusalem Falls to Crusaders	26

K

Kennedy, John	18
Khan, Genghis	13, 48
King Arthur	20
King James Bible	21
King, Martin Luther Jr.	16, 44
Kites, First	12

L

League of Nations	20
Leaning Tower of Pisa	19, 35
Leif Ericsson Discovers North America	24, 37
Lenin, Vladimir	13, 50
Lewis & Clark Expedition	14, 46
Lincoln, Abraham	17
Louisiana Purchase	15

Louis XIV of France	21
Lusitania Sinks	25, 41
Luther, Martin	23, 35

M

Madagascar Settled by French	11
Madison, James	17
Magellan, Ferdinand	23, 35
Magna Carta Signed	19, 37
Magnetic Compass	12, 49
Magnifying Glass	19, 36
Machine Gun	25
Manchu Dynasty	13
Man Walks on Moon	16, 44
Marx, Karl	13
Mary Queen of Scots	20, 38
Mass Production of Books	12
Mayan Calendar	14
Mayan Golden Age	14
McKinley, William	18
Michelangelo Buonarroti	23, 39
Mickey Mouse Cartoon	16
Microscope Invented	21
Middle Kingdom	11, 51
Ming Dynasty	13, 48
Miracle of Dunkirk	24
Modern Globe	23
Mohammed (Muhammad)	26, 47
Mongol Empire	13
Mongul Empire	13, 48
Monroe Doctrine	16, 46
Monroe, James	17
Movable Type Used (Europe)	19
Mummies	11, 50
Munich Agreement	24, 42
Mussolini, Benito	24, 42

N

NATO	24
Nero	20, 32
New Deal	15, 45
New Holy Roman Empire	24
New Kingdom	11, 51
Newton, Isaac	21, 38
Nightingale, Florence	24
Nixon, Richard	18
North Kingdom of Israel Destroyed	26
Northwest Ordinance	15, 47

O

Octavian	22, 34
Old Kingdom, Egypt	11, 50
Olympic Games	20, 32
Opium War	13, 50
Otto I of Germany	24, 37
Ottoman Empire	26, 47

P

Panama Canal	16, 44
Paper First Made (Europe)	19
Papyrus Used as Paper	11
Parchment	26
Parthenon	22, 33
Peloponnesian War	22, 32
Persian Gulf War	26

People's Republic of China	13
Persecution, First	20
Persian War	22, 33
Peter the Great	13, 48
Pharaoh Menes	11, 50
Philip II	20, 33
Picasso, Pablo	19, 41
Pierce, Franklin	17
Pilgrim's Progress	21, 38
Pilgrims Reach Cape Cod	14
Plato	22, 33
Poison Gas Used in War	25
Polio Vaccination	15
Polk, James	17
Polo, Marco	19, 35
Pony Express	15, 46
Popes Dominated by French	19
Pope, First	20
Pope George VII Challenges Henry IV	24
Pope Nicholas I	24
Pottery Figures	12
Prayer Removed from Schools	15
Prohibition	15
Ptolemy	20
Punic War	22, 34
Puritan Revolution (England)	21
Pyramids	11, 50
Pythagoras	21

Q

Quakers Settled Pennsylvania	15
Queen Elizabeth	23, 39

R

Radio Broadcasting in U.S.	16, 44
Raleigh, Sir Walter	19
Reagan, Ronald	18
Reformation Starts	21, 38
Resettlement of Israel	26
Revolutionary War	14, 43
Richard the Lion Hearted	19, 35
Rockets Used in Battle	13
Roman Emperor, Last Dethroned	20
Roman Empire	22, 34
Roman Empire Divided	22
Rome Destroyed by Fire	22
Roosevelt, Franklin	18
Roosevelt, Theodore	18
Russo-Japanese War	13, 48

S

Salem Witch Trials	14, 42
Salvation Army	16, 46
Samurai	12, 48
Scientific Revolution	23
Seven Years' War	25, 40
Sequoya	16
Shakespeare, William	23, 39
Shang Dynasty	12, 49
Silk Paintings	12
Socrates	22, 33
Song Dynasty	13
Space Shuttle	15
Spain Established	23
Spanish Armada Defeated	21

Spanish Civil War	25, 42
Spanish Inquisition	23
Sphinx	11, 50
Statue of Liberty	16, 44
St. Francis of Assisi	19, 36
Stonehenge	20, 32
Suez Canal	11, 51
Surgery, First (Egypt)	11
Surgery, First (Europe)	21

T

Taft, William	18
Taj Mahal Built	13, 48
T'ang Dynasty	12, 49
Tanks Used in Battle	25
Taylor, Zachary	17
Telephone	15, 47
Tenochtitlan Founded	14
Thirty Years' War	21, 38
Titanic Sinks	15, 45
Traffic Lights	16
Transcontinental Railroad	15, 46
Treaty of Paris	14, 43
Treaty of Verdun	24, 37
Treaty of Versailles	25, 41
Triple Alliance	25, 41
Triple Entente	25, 41
Trojan War	20, 32
Truman, Harry	18
Tyler, John	17
Tyndale, William	21

U

U.S. Stock Market Crashes	16
U.S. War With Mexico	15

V

Van Buren, Martin	17
Vikings Settle Iceland	24
Virginia Colony Founded	14

W

War of the Roses	21
Washington, Booker T.	15, 46
Washington, George	14
Watch, First	23
Wesley, John	22, 42
Wheels First Used	26
William the Conqueror	24, 37
Wilson, Woodrow	18
Windmills First Used	26
Wooden Blocks for Printing (China)	13
World War I	25, 41
World War II	25, 42
Writing Appears	26
Wycliffe, John	21, 36

Y

YMCA Founded	24

About the Author:

Liberty Wiggers (Libby) is a home school graduate of the class of 1999. These timeline figures are the result of a year long history project. She originally printed the figures on a laser printer and packaged them in poly storage bags; however, she sold so many through the family business (Geography Matters) the first year that she was able to publish a professionally printed and bound version, saving her loads of time once used to print, collate and bag. Not only did this project provided Libby a better understanding of the flow of history, but she also became very proficient in the use of the Quark Express and Photoshop computer programs she used to design the figures.

On a personal note, she is proud to call herself a Christian, loves to read classic and historical novels, collects anything with dalmations and plans to pursue the study of biology and chemistry in college. She sets aside all profits from the sales of her book for college tuition.

Other Fine Products from Geography Matters, Inc.
Ordering information
Wholesale accounts welcomed.

The Mark-It Timeline of History - $9.95
This is the poster-sized double-sided activity timeline for which these timeline figures were designed. Dated from B.C. 4000 to 2050 A.D. on the front and undated on the back, your students fill out the details throughout the school year(s). Laminated for durability you can write directly on the time line using Vis-a Vis overhead projector pens. Figures are easy to move and remove on the laminated surface. 24" x 34".

The Ultimate Geography and Timeline Guide, 353 pages - $34.95
Need more detailed instructions on using outline maps, teaching geography and incorporating geography while studying other subjects? This is your answer! Packed with lesson plans, reproducibles, and activities geared for grades K-12.

Uncle Josh's Outline Map Book, 112 pages - $19.95
Over 100 quality outline maps of the U.S. and world. Includes one of each of the U.S. states, each continent and major countries and regions of the world. Reproducible. Rivers are lightly shaded and longitude and latitude grid lines are drawn where possible.

Historical Timeline Figures, 100 pages - $25.00

Shipping and handling charges: Orders up to $50.00 add $5.00 for shipping
                                  Orders over $50.00 add 10%

Call for a complete catalog, or check out our web site for catalog and printable online activities. To order items on this page send check or money order with shipping included to:

Geography Matters
P.O. Box 92
Nancy, KY 42544

(800) 426-4650   *www.geomatters.com*